Women in
STEM
CHEMISTRY
Edited by Jane Dunne
LIGHTBOX
openlightbox.com

Lightbox is an all-inclusive digital solution for the teaching and learning of curriculum topics in an original, groundbreaking way. Lightbox is based on National Curriculum Standards.

STANDARD FEATURES OF LIGHTBOX

AUDIO High-quality narration using text-to-speech system

ACTIVITIES Printable PDFs that can be emailed and graded

SLIDESHOWS Pictorial overviews of key concepts

VIDEOS Embedded high-definition video clips

WEBLINKS Curated links to external, child-safe resources

TRANSPARENCIES Step-by-step layering of maps, diagrams, charts, and timelines

INTERACTIVE MAPS Interactive maps and aerial satellite imagery

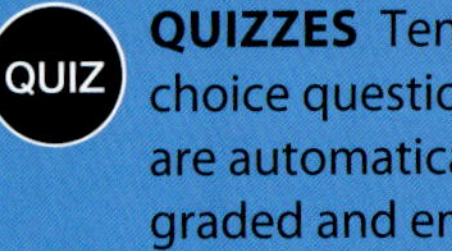

QUIZZES Ten multiple choice questions that are automatically graded and emailed for teacher assessment

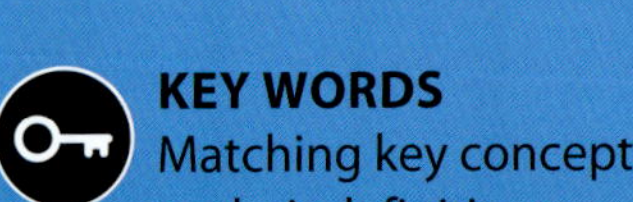

KEY WORDS Matching key concepts to their definitions

Women in STEM

CHEMISTRY

CONTENTS

Women in Chemistry

In the science of chemistry, people study the substances and processes that make up everything in the world. Scientists look at the way **matter** is made up from atoms and **molecules**. They study how substances behave, and how they change and interact with each other. Chemistry involves different fields, or specialities. Chemists focus on different things, such as medicine, technology, and the environment.

About one million years ago, people realized they could use fire to change one substance into another. Two hundred thousand years ago, there is archaeological evidence to show that humans were using fire to make weapons and cook food. Both women and men did this. Five thousand years ago, people had discovered how to melt and mix metals with other metals. Tin was added to copper to make bronze, which was harder than pure tin or copper.

By the Middle Ages, people called **alchemists** believed that matter could be turned into other substances. They tried to find ways of mixing different substances together to make gold. Some of these alchemists were women.

Alchemists were often thought to have magical powers. Women involved in alchemy during the medieval period were sometimes persecuted for being witches.

An Egyptian woman is said to have invented the alembic. This was a tool used for heating substances so they could be separated into different parts. The work of alchemists paved the way for the development of early modern science. By the late-1800s, women in Europe and North America had made exciting discoveries in chemistry. In 1870, Ellen Swallow Richards became the first U.S. chemistry graduate. In the same year, Anna Volkova became the first woman to graduate as a chemist in Russia.

The alembic was a container with a cap and a long tube that connected it to another container. Similar tools are used by chemists today.

Today, a term is used to describe and group together the major fields of science. These are science, technology, engineering, and mathematics, or STEM. Women have had to fight to overcome **prejudice** in some of these fields, but the number of women involved in biological sciences now exceeds that of men. Many women have become leaders in their scientific fields, and continue to inspire new generations.

STEM DEGREES EARNED BY WOMEN IN THE UNITED STATES—2016

	BACHELOR'S	MASTER'S	PhD
Biological and biomedical	59.9%	57.3%	53%
Math and statistics	42.5%	41.7%	28.5%
Physical science and technology	38.8%	37.8%	32.2%
Engineering and technology	19.7%	25.2%	23.5%
Computer and information science	18.7%	30.8%	20.1%
All STEM fields	**35.5%**	**32.6%**	**33.7%**

Chemistry Worldwide

For centuries, alchemy had been practiced in Ancient Greece, Egypt, and Asia. It had been based partly on ancient beliefs about magic. By the 1600s, many alchemists and scientists in Europe recognized that such beliefs needed to be proven using **scientific method**. Alchemy had paved the way for the new science of chemistry.

Chemistry began to be taught in universities across the world. However, until the late 1800s, it was hard for women to become chemists in North America and Europe. Until then, women were not allowed to study at universities. Many women chemists, such as Agnes Pockels, began their scientific lives carrying out experiments at home. When universities finally began to admit women, many of them made discoveries that changed the world.

Arctic Ocean
Paris, France
Marie Curie had to leave her home in Poland to study science in Paris. It is here that she became one of the best known scientists in history. In 1911, she was awarded the Nobel Prize for her discovery of new elements and experiments with **radiation**.
Brunswick, Germany
Agnes Pockels spent most of her life in Brunswick as a homemaker looking after her parents. She noticed how oils, dirt, and soaps floated on the surface of the water she used to wash dishes. She invented a tool to measure their effects on the water surface.
Atlantic Ocean
EUROPE
ASIA
Pacific Ocean
Indian Ocean
AFRICA
Bianjing, China
In the tenth century, Chinese alchemist Keng Hsien-Seng was skilled in heating and cooling metals. She was an expert at extracting silver from ores, and was said to be able to create silver from mercury.
Venice, Italy
In 1561, a book called *The Secrets of Lady Isabella Cortese*, was published. Written by Isabella Cortese, an Italian alchemist, it contained medical remedies and instructions on how to make glue, toothpaste, soap, and polish. It even described how to make gold. The book was popular and reprinted many times between 1561 and 1677.
MAP LEGEND
Land
Water
N
SCALE
0
1,000 miles
1,000 kilometers
Southern Ocean
ANTARCTICA

Ellen Swallow Richards

Name: Ellen Swallow Richards
Born: 1842, Dunstable, Massachusetts
Died: 1911, Jamaica Plain, Massachusetts
Occupation: Environmental chemist
Education: Vassar College and Massachusetts Institute of Technology (MIT)
Major discoveries and achievements: Improved water quality in the United States
Major honors: President of the American Home Economics Association, Ellen Swallow Richards chair at MIT named for her

Ellen was educated at home by her parents, who were both teachers. Her family was not wealthy. She became a tutor, teaching French and German to earn enough money to attend Vassar College in New York State. After graduating, she was admitted to the Massachusetts Institute of Technology (MIT) in 1871. She was the first woman in America to enter a scientific school.

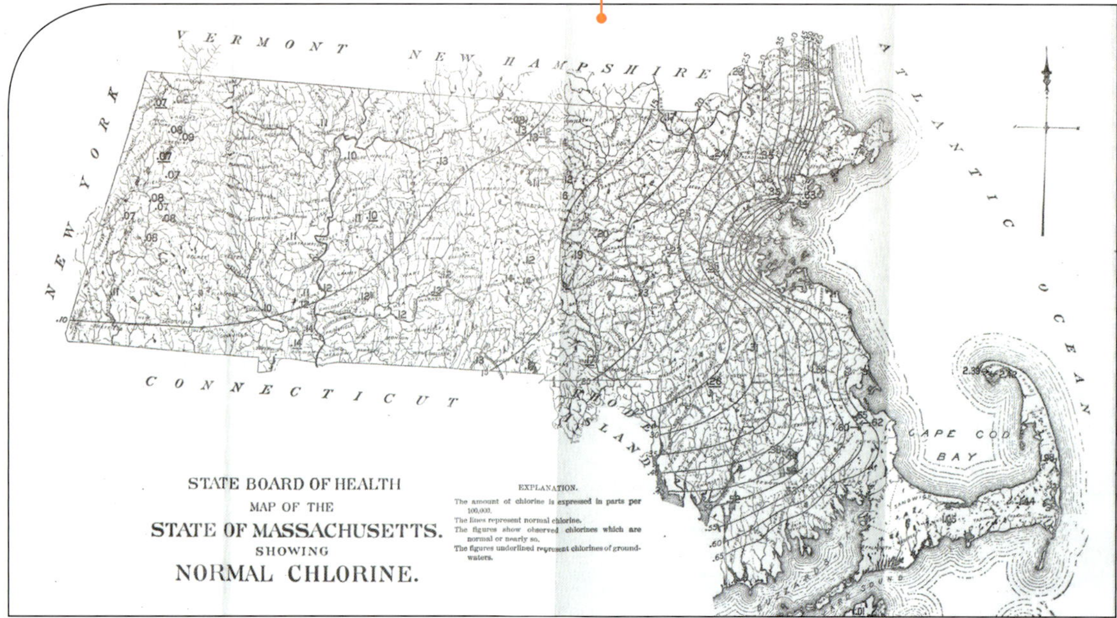

Ellen made a detailed study of the chlorine in drinking water from all water sources in Massachusetts. This helped the state to map the pollution of water.

Ellen Swallow Richards taught subjects such as chemical analysis, mineralogy, and industrial chemistry at the MIT Women's Laboratory.

Ellen married Robert Richards in 1875. He was head of the Mine Engineering Department at MIT. Robert helped Ellen to set up a Women's Laboratory at MIT, which offered practical chemistry experience for women chemists. In 1883, Ellen became the assistant chemist at MIT's laboratory of sanitary chemistry. She tested 40,000 water samples from all over the state of Massachusetts. She traced the amount of chlorine in these samples. As a result, Massachusetts set up the first modern sewage treatment plant.

Ellen was enthusiastic about applying scientific principles to all aspects of life. In 1882, she wrote *The Chemistry of Cooking and Cleaning: A Manual for Housekeepers*. Subjects covered included nutrition, cleaning, and sanitation. The book contributed to the development of the practical science of home economics.

THE DAWN OF MODERN CHEMISTRY

Robert Boyle experimented with gases during the 1600s. He is famous for discovering "Boyle's Law." This describes how the pressure of gas increases as the volume of its container decreases.

In the late 1700s, Joseph Priestley discovered that a mysterious gas supported **combustion** more effectively than ordinary air. This gas was later called oxygen. Its discovery helped the French chemist, Antoine Lavoisier.

Antoine Lavoisier used Priestley's theories to discover that oxygen makes up about 20 percent of air. He realized that oxygen was essential for both combustion and breathing.

Humphrey Davy used electricity to separate many **elements.** These included potassium and magnesium. He invented a "safety lamp" for miners that would not ignite the methane in coal mines.

Jöns Jacob Berzelius worked in the early 1800s. He discovered the **atomic weight** of elements. He also invented the system of chemical symbols called the periodic table used by scientists today.

Agnes Pockels

Name: Agnes Pockels
Born: 1862, Venice, Italy
Died: 1935, Brunswick, Germany
Occupation: Chemist and housekeeper
Education: No formal science education
Major discoveries and achievements: Opened up the study of **surface science**, invented the "Pockels trough" for measuring **surface tension**
Major honors: The Laura Leonard Award in 1931, honorary doctorate from the Technical University of Brunswick, Germany, in 1932

When Agnes Pockels was born, her father was serving with the Austrian army. When he fell ill, the family moved to Brunswick, in Germany. Agnes attended the local girls' high school, but was not allowed to study science. The best she could do was to read the books her parents bought for her younger brother, Friedrich. He studied science and later became a physicist.

Pockels spent much of her younger life housekeeping for her parents. She was fascinated by the way different substances floated on water. This was particularly noticeable when she was washing dishes. She observed that matter such as oils, fats, dirt, and soap behaved differently. She also noticed that these different substances formed thin films on the surface of the water. These films varied in thickness, depending on the substance.

Agnes Pockels was fascinated by the interaction of water and other materials. Her curiosity led her to create an important piece of equipment to measure this.

Agnes was not happy just to watch what was happening. She wanted to carry out experiments and record the results. She set up a simple device in her kitchen, which was later known as "Pockels trough." First, she filled a rectangular tray with water. Then, she divided the trough by putting a thin, moveable strip of metal across the surface of the water. When she added oil to one side of the strip and pulled the strip across the water, it changed the surface tension. Agnes also tried this experiment with wax.

Friedrich was studying physics at the University of Göttingen. Knowing that his sister was interested in surface tension, he gave her a copy of a paper written by the British physicist, Lord Rayleigh. Friedrich also encouraged Agnes to write to Lord Rayleigh about her work. Rayleigh was astonished by her findings, and persuaded *Nature* magazine to publish her letter in an article entitled "Surface Tension."

Pockels became internationally famous for her experiments. However, the death of her brother, and then the outbreak of World War I (1914–1918), interrupted her work. After the war, failing eyesight limited her experiments.

During World War I, in 1917, American chemist Irving Langmuir used a version of Pockels trough to carry out similar experiments. He worked out how and why oil floats on water. He won the Nobel Prize in Chemistry in 1932.

The way soap bubbles reacted with oils, fats, and water made Pockels keen to understand the chemistry behind the interactions.

Dishwashing detergent sales worldwide are worth more than **$10 billion** per year.

Marie Curie

Name: Marie Curie
Born: 1867, Warsaw, Poland
Died: 1934, Haute-Savoie, France
Occupation: Chemist
Education: Sorbonne, Paris
Major discoveries and achievements: Discovery of the elements polonium and radium, research into **radioactivity**
Major honors: Nobel Prize in Physics, 1903; Nobel Prize in Chemistry, 1911

Marie Sklodowska was the fifth child of parents who were teachers. As a child, she loved science, and her family encouraged her interest. Poland was under Russian rule at the time, and it was difficult for Marie to continue her studies. She took up the offer of a place at the Sorbonne University in Paris, and moved to France when she was 24 years old. She was one of only a few women among 2,000 men. After graduation, she stayed in Paris and married a fellow scientist, Pierre Curie.

Marie Curie invented the term radioactivity. She realized that radiation must be coming from within atoms themselves. This was a revolutionary idea.

Pierre had invented a version of a machine called an electrometer, which measured electrical charges in the air. Marie used this device to measure the electricity in the air around uranium. She worked on the minerals pitchblende and torbernite and, in 1898, discovered that the pitchblende was giving off unexpectedly strong radiation. She realized that she had discovered another new radioactive element. She named it polonium, after her native Poland. Later that year, the Curies announced that they had found another element in pitchblende. This was radium.

Pierre Curie recognized that Marie's work was important. They worked closely together from 1898.

In 1903, Marie and Pierre, along with fellow scientist Henri Becquerel, were awarded the Nobel Prize in Physics for their research into radiation. Pierre became professor of physics at the University of Paris, but in 1906, he was knocked down and killed by a horse-drawn carriage. Marie was given Pierre's job at the university, and continued the work they had begun together.

In 1911, Marie was awarded the Nobel Prize in Chemistry for the discovery of radium. She was the first person to be awarded the Nobel Prize in two fields of science—physics and chemistry. Marie carried on her research into radiation until she died from leukemia in 1934.

IRÈNE JOLIOT-CURIE

Irène Joliot Curie (1897–1956) was the daughter of Pierre and Marie Curie. She studied science at the Sorbonne, and then worked as a nurse during World War I. She pioneered a method of using x-rays to locate **shrapnel** in the bodies of injured soldiers. In 1926, she married the scientist Frédéric Joliot. In 1934, she and her husband worked out how to change the central particles in atoms to create a different, radioactive element. They won the Nobel Prize in Chemistry in 1935 for this discovery, which was a stepping stone in the development of nuclear power. Irène worked for the French atomic energy commission after World War II, and also ran the Curie Institute in Paris. She died from leukemia, which was probably caused by exposure to polonium.

Irène Joliot-Curie carried on her mother's work and helped establish peaceful uses for radioactivity.

Rachel Fuller Brown

Name: Rachel Fuller Brown
Born: 1898, Springfield, Massachusetts
Died: 1980, Albany, New York
Occupation: Chemist
Education: Mount Holyoke College, University of Chicago
Major discoveries and achievements: Creating effective medicines to attack diseases caused by fungi, discovering different types of pneumonia
Major honors: Fellow of the New York Academy of Sciences, American Institute of Chemists' Chemical Pioneer Award.

Rachel Fuller Brown's father left the family in 1912, and her mother had to find work to try and support the family. Rachel was a good school student, but it looked like there would not be enough money to send her to college. Fortunately, Rachel received a small scholarship to attend Mount Holyoke College. A wealthy relative paid the rest of her tuition fees.

Elizabeth Lee Hazen and Rachel Fuller Brown spent years testing samples to find a bacteria that would attack fungal infections.

Penicillin was a drug used in World War II to protect wounded soldiers from infection. Penicillin saved lives, but side effects included an increase in fungal infections.

Fungal infections of the skin are the world's **fourth most common disease,** affecting almost **1 billion people.**

1.6 MILLION people die each year from **fungal infections.**

Rachel majored in history and chemistry and graduated in 1920. She went on to gain a master's degree in organic chemistry from the University of Chicago. Afterward, she taught science at a private school to earn enough money to fund her PhD. In 1924, she was able to return to the University of Chicago, where she took a doctorate degree in chemistry and bacteriology.

After leaving university, Rachel's first job was as a medical researcher in Albany. She worked on finding ways to screen people for syphilis. Syphilis is a serious disease that can kill people if it is left untreated. She also discovered 40 types of pneumonia, which is an infection of the lungs, and developed different **antiserums** that could be used to treat these types of pneumonia.

In 1948, Rachel began work on an important project. In the aftermath of World War II, many war veterans were found to have fungal infections. This was partly a result of the use of penicillin, which encouraged fungal growth. There was no known cure for these infections. Rachel worked to find fungus-fighting bacteria with Elizabeth Lee Hazen. Hazen sent soil samples containing bacteria to Rachel, who tested them.

After two years, a bacteria was found that successfully cured fungal infections. It came from a farm in New York State. The discovery was **patented** as "Nystatin." The profits from the sale of the drug were used to set up the Brown–Hazen Research Fund, which gave educational grants to young scientists.

Dorothy Hodgkin

Name: Dorothy Crowfoot Hodgkin
Born: 1910, Cairo, Egypt
Died: 1980, Albany, New York
Occupation: Chemist
Education: Oxford University, Cambridge University
Major discoveries and achievements: Developing protein crystallography, finding the structure of insulin
Major honors: Nobel Prize in Chemistry, 1964; the Order of Merit, 1965; the Copley Medal, 1976

After spending her first few years of life in Egypt, Dorothy moved to Great Britain with her family when World War I broke out in 1914. At about the age of 10, Dorothy became fascinated by minerals and crystals. She was one of just two girls who were allowed to study chemistry at her school in Beccles. Dorothy went on to receive a first-class chemistry degree from Oxford University, and then studied for her PhD at Cambridge. She was interested in **x-ray** crystallography. This was a developing area of science in which x-rays showed scientists the 3-D structure of molecules.

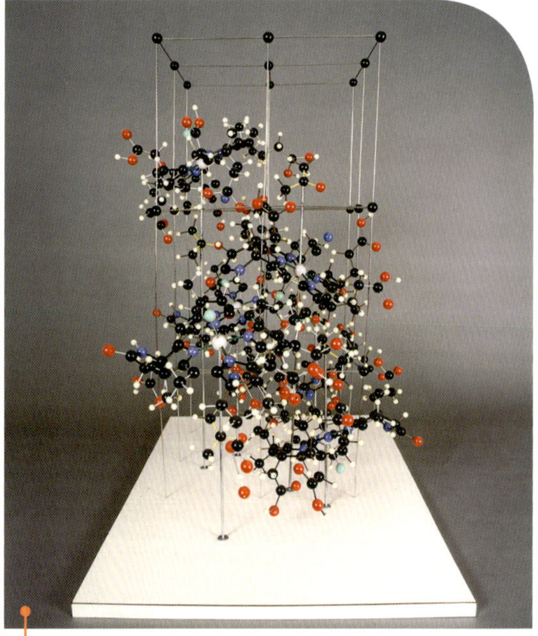

In 1958, a model of the structure of vitamin B12 was made from Dorothy's x-ray crystallography imaging.

During the 1940s, Dorothy worked on the structure of penicillin and, in 1945, made a model showing its molecular structure. This work was not published until 1949. Her results were important for research into other molecules, such as **DNA**. Dorothy's most important discovery was the structure of vitamin B12. This vitamin is vital for health. By showing the structures of penicillin and vitamin B12, Dorothy had made it possible to make lifesaving drugs. Scientists could also alter the structures to make better drugs.

Dorothy continued to work until late in her life. She won many awards for her achievements.

Another complex molecule that Dorothy uncovered was insulin. She had first studied it in 1935. However, it was not until 1969 that the structure of insulin was finally understood. Insulin is important in the treatment of diabetes.

Dorothy spent much of her working life at Oxford University, where she inspired many younger scientists. Dorothy believed that scientists had responsibilities to society. From 1976 to 1988, she was chairwoman of the Pugwash Movement, which is an international organization founded by scientists in 1957. Its aim is to promote the peaceful use of scientific discoveries and reduce the dangers of armed conflict.

INSULIN AND DIABETES

Diabetes is one of the most common diseases in the world. Up to five million people die from diabetes each year. Before the 1960s, it was difficult to make enough insulin to help people. Most insulin was made from the bodies of animals, but it took many hundreds of animals to make a very small amount of insulin. Dorothy's discovery of the structure of the insulin molecule was a major step forward. It led the way toward scientists making synthetic, or human-made, insulin for medical use. Using her discovery, medical scientists developed a new form of insulin, called Humulin, in 1982.

Rosalind Franklin

Name: Rosalind Elsie Franklin
Born: 1920, London, Great Britain
Died: 1958, London, Great Britain
Occupation: Chemist
Education: Cambridge University, Great Britain
Major discoveries and achievements: Helping to discover the structure of DNA, coal, and **viruses**

Rosalind Franklin knew she wanted to be a scientist from the age of 15. As a young girl, she was gifted in languages, as well as math and science. In 1938, Rosalind went to study at Newnham College, Cambridge, in Great Britain, and graduated in 1941. From 1942 to the end of 1945, she worked as a scientist at the British Coal Utilisation research Association. She studied the properties of coal and carbon, classifying different types of coal and analyzing how they would behave under different conditions. In 1947, this work led to a job in Paris at the Laboratoire Central des Services Chimique de l'Etat. Here, she used x-ray crystallography to study the molecules of carbon.

In 1951, Rosalind returned to Britain. She became a researcher at King's College, London. The head of the laboratory, John Randall, asked her to look at the structure of DNA, about which little was known.

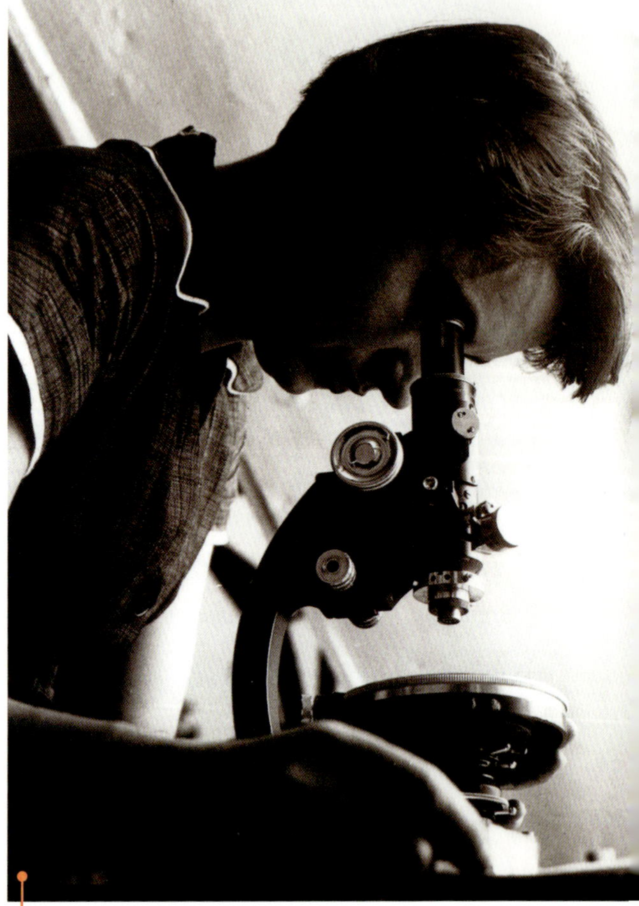

Rosalind's work led to an understanding of the structure of the DNA molecule.

Rosalind took x-ray images of DNA. She realized that DNA had two forms, one wet and one dry. She noticed a **helix** structure in the wet form of DNA. One of her colleagues, Maurice Wilkins, showed one of the x-ray images, known as Photo 51, to two researchers at Cambridge University. They were Frances Crick and James Watson, and they were also studying the structure of DNA.

The helix that Rosalind had recognized confirmed the ideas of a double helix that Crick and Watson were developing. In 1953, they published their results in *Nature* magazine. The paper owed much to Rosalind's own work, but Crick and Watson did not acknowledge her contribution until much later. Rosalind was a cautious researcher. She did not believe that the double helix structure of DNA could be proven on the evidence then available.

Franklin continued her crystallography work at Birkbeck College, London. She studied viruses, in particular those that attacked plants. Her final work involved trying to discover the structure of the virus that caused polio, or infantile paralysis. After her death, one of her assistants, Aaron Klug, won the Nobel Prize in Chemistry for this work.

Rosalind Franklin died from ovarian cancer in 1958, aged just 37. Only after her death was her contribution to the mystery of DNA finally recognized.

Maurice Wilkins was Rosalind Franklin's colleague at King's College, London. He shared her findings that confirmed the double helix structure of DNA.

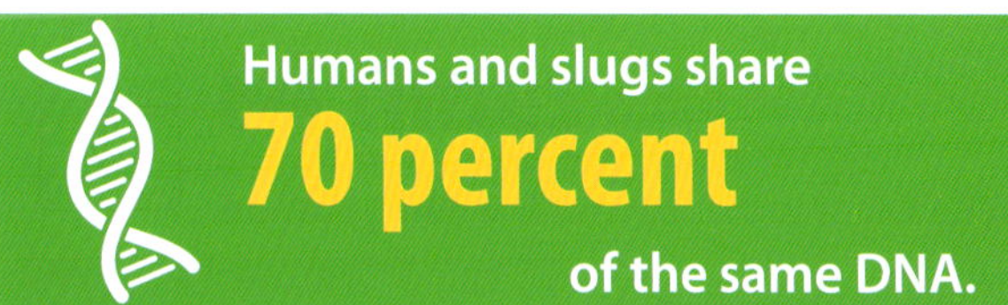

Every human on the planet shares **99.9 percent** of the same DNA.

Timeline of Chemistry

Before the late 1800s, women who wanted to be scientists had to fight hard to follow their dream. They could help other family members, but many educational institutions did not allow women to study. Even universities that admitted women believed the only scientific subjects women should be studying were domestic science and cooking. Only after many struggles were women completely accepted. Today, more women than ever before are choosing careers in chemistry.

1800 | 1850 | 1900 | 1910 | 1930

1808
Anna Persdotter, later Sundström, begins to work for Swedish chemistry pioneer Jöns Jacob Berzelius. She ran his laboratory and supervised his students.

1870
Anna Volkova is the first woman to graduate as a chemist, in Saint Petersburg, Russia.

1882
Ellen Swallow Richards publishes her best-selling book *The Chemistry of Cooking and Cleaning.*

1891
Nature magazine publishes Agnes Pockels' article on "Surface Tension."

1911
Marie Curie wins the Nobel Prize in Chemistry for her discovery of radium and polonium.

In a chemistry research laboratory, the results of experiments have to be checked, and then double-checked. This is part of the scientific method. Women scientists are at the forefront of such scientific research today.

1950 | 1970 | 1980 | 2000 | 2018

1953
Rosalind Franklin suggests that DNA has the structure of a double helix.

1969
Dorothy Hodgkin discovers the molecular structure of insulin, after more than 30 years of research.

1975
Rachel Fuller Brown receives the American Institute of Chemists' Chemical Pioneer Award for her work in discovering effective anti-fungal treatments.

2018
Frances Arnold is awarded the Nobel Prize in Chemistry for her work in engineering the evolution of **enzymes**.

Quiz

1 What were the medieval scientists who tried to create gold from other metals called?

2 In which U.S. state did Ellen Swallow Richards collect 40,000 water samples?

3 What practical science did Ellen Swallow Richards contribute to?

4 How did Agnes Pockels teach herself about science?

5 What piece of apparatus did Agnes Pockels invent?

6 What disease did Marie Curie and her daughter die from?

7 What was a side effect of the widespread use of penicillin in World War II?

8 What is the common name of the anti-fungal infection drug that Rachel Fuller Brown helped create?

9 What did it take Dorothy Hodgkin 34 years to discover?

10 What photographic technique did Rosalind Franklin use to make an image of DNA?

ANSWERS

1. Alchemists **2.** Massachusetts **3.** Home economics **4.** From books brought home by her younger brother **5.** The "Pockels trough" **6.** Leukemia, probably caused by exposure to radioactive elements **7.** An increase in fungal infections **8.** Nystatin **9.** The structure of insulin **10.** X-rays

Key Words

alchemists: scientists from the Middle Ages who tried to change metals into gold

antiserums: blood serums containing antibodies to treat specific diseases

atomic weight: the total number of protons and neutrons in an atom

combustion: a chemical reaction that produces heat and light

DNA: substance that carries genetic information in the cells of living things

elements: pure substances that cannot be broken up. Elements contain only one type of atom.

enzymes: substances that speed up chemical reactions in plants and animals

helix: an object with a 3-D shape like a wire around a cylinder, or a spiral staircase

matter: substance that everything physical is made from

molecules: the smallest amounts of substances that still have the properties of that substance

patented: obtained the exclusive rights to an invention or process

prejudice: hatred or unfair treatment toward a person or group of people without cause

radiation: high-energy waves from the Sun or nuclear power, which cause sunburn or other tissue damage in the body

radioactivity: the emission of powerful, harmful energy

scientific method: carrying out observations and experiments based on predictions, and recording the results

shrapnel: fragments of metal or other objects thrown out by an explosion, usually in war

surface science: study of what happens when two states, such as liquid and oil or gas, come into contact with each other

surface tension: a force in the surface layer of a liquid that causes the layer to behave like an elastic sheet

viruses: tiny particles that cause disease and can spread from one person or animal to another

x-ray: invisible light ray that can pass through an object; also, an image made using these rays that shows the inside of something

Index

LIGHTBOX

SUPPLEMENTARY RESOURCES

Click on the plus icon found in the bottom left corner of each spread to open additional teacher resources.

- Download and print the book's quizzes and activities
- Access curriculum correlations
- Explore additional web applications that enhance the Lightbox experience

LIGHTBOX DIGITAL TITLES
Packed full of integrated media

VIDEOS

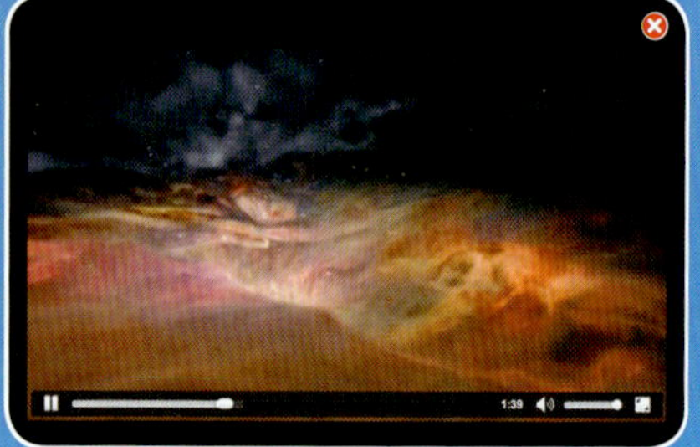

INTERACTIVE MAPS

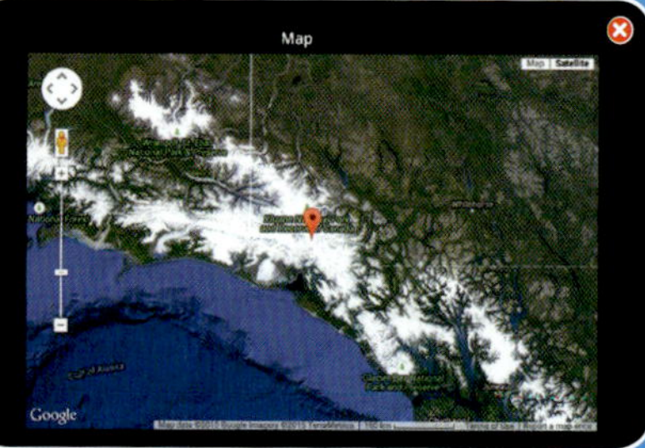

WEBLINKS

SLIDESHOWS

QUIZZES

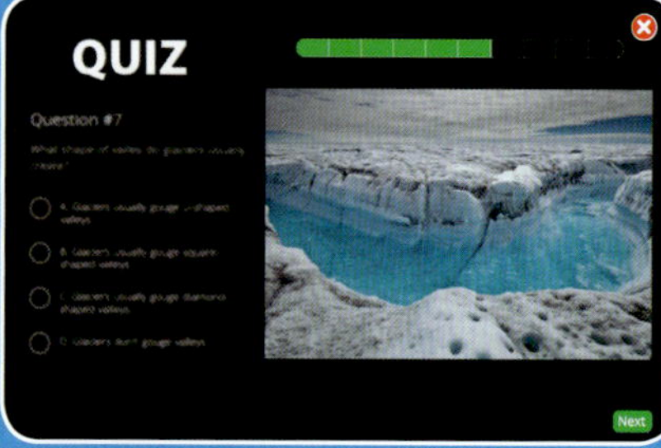

OPTIMIZED FOR

- ✓ TABLETS
- ✓ WHITEBOARDS
- ✓ COMPUTERS
- ✓ AND MUCH MORE!

Published by Smartbook Media Inc.
350 5th Avenue, 59th Floor New York, NY 10118
Website: www.openlightbox.com

Project Coordinator: Heather Kissock
Art Director: Terry Paulhus

Library of Congress Control Number: 2019942199

ISBN 978-1-5105-4425-3 (hardcover)
ISBN 978-1-5105-4426-0 (multi-user eBook)

Printed in Guangzhou, China
1 2 3 4 5 6 7 8 9 0 23 22 21 20 19

072019
311218

Photo Credits
Every reasonable effort has been made to trace ownership and to obtain permission to reprint copyright material. The publisher would be pleased to have any errors or omissions brought to its attention so that they may be corrected in subsequent printings.

The publisher acknowledges Getty Images, Alamy, and Shutterstock as its primary image suppliers for this title.